On The Ruin of Britain (De Excidio Britanniae)

by

Gildas

Translation by J. A. Giles

The Works of Gildas surnamed "Sapiens", or The Wise.

I. The Preface

1. Whatever in this my epistle I may write in my humble but well meaning manner, rather by way of lamentation than for display, let no one suppose that it springs from contempt of others or that I foolishly esteem myself as better than they; -for alas! the subject of my complaint is the general destruction of every thing that is good, and the general growth of evil throughout the land; —but that I rejoice to see her revive therefrom: for it is my present purpose to relate the deeds of an indolent and slothful race, rather than the exploits of those who have been valiant in the field*. I have kept silence, I confess, with much mental anguish, compunction of feeling and contrition of heart, whilst I revolved all these things within myself; and, as God the searcher of the reins is witness, for the space of even ten years or more, [my inexperience, as at present also, and my unworthiness preventing me from taking upon myself the character of a censor. But I read how the illustrious lawgiver, for one word's doubting, was not allowed to enter the desired land; that the sons of the high-priest, for placing strange fire upon God's altar, were cut off by a speedy death; that God's people, for breaking the law of God, save two only, were slain by wild beasts, by fire and sword in the deserts of Arabia, though God had so loved them that he had made a way for them through the Red Sea, had fed

them with bread from heaven, and water from the rock, and by the lifting up of a hand merely had made their armies invincible; and then, when they had crossed the Jordan and entered the unknown land, and the walls of the city had fallen down flat at the sound only of a trumpet, the taking of a cloak and a little gold from the accursed things caused the deaths of many: and again the breach of their treaty with the Gibeonites, though that treaty had been obtained by fraud, brought destruction upon many; and I took warning from the sins of the people which called down upon them the reprehensions of the prophets and also of Jeremiah, with his fourfold Lamentations written in alphabetical order. I saw moreover in my own time, as that prophet also had complained, that the city had sat down lone and widowed, which before was full of people; that the queen of nations and the princess of provinces (i. e. the church), had been made tributary; that the gold was obscured, and the most excellent colour (which is the brightness of God's word) changed; that the sons of Sion (i. e. of holy mother church), once famous and clothed in the finest gold, grovelled in dung; and what added intolerably to the weight of grief of that illustrious man, and to mine, though but an abject, whilst he had thus mourned them in their happy and prosperous condition, "Her Nazarites were fairer than snow, more ruddy than old ivory, more beautiful than the saphire. " These and many other passages in the ancient Scriptures I regarded as a kind of mirror of human life, and I turned also to the New, wherein I read more clearly what perhaps to me before was dark, for the darkness fled, and truth shed her steady light-I read therein that the Lord had said, "I came not but to the lost sheep of the house of Israel; " and on the other hand, "But the children of this kingdom shall be cast out into outer darkness; there shall be weeping and gnashing of teeth: " and again, "It is not good to take the children's meat and to give it to dogs: " also, "Woe to you, scribes and pharisees, hypocrites! " I heard how "many shall come from the east and the west and shall sit down with Abraham, Isaac, and Jacob in the kingdom of heaven: " and on the contrary, "I will then say to them 'Depart from me, ye workers of iniquity! '" I read, "Blessed are the barren and the teats which have not given suck; " and on the contrary, "Those, who were ready, entered with him to the wedding; afterwards came the other virgins also, saying 'Lord, Lord, open to us: ' to whom it was answered, 'I do not know you. '" I heard, forsooth, "Whoever shall believe and be baptized, shall be saved, but whoever shall not believe shall be damned." I read in the words of the apostle that the branch of the wild olive was grafted upon the good olive, but should nevertheless be cut off from the communion of the root of its fatness, if it did not hold itself in fear, but entertained lofty thoughts. I knew the mercy of the Lord, but I also feared his judgment: I praised his grace, but I feared the rendering to every man according to his works: perceiving the sheep of the same fold to be different, I deservedly commended Peter for his entire confession of Christ, but called Judas most wretched, for his love of covetousness: I thought Stephen most glorious on account of the palm of martyrdom, but Nicholas wretched for his mark of unclean heresy: I read assuredly, "They had all things common: " but likewise also, as it is written, "Why have ye conspired to tempt the Spirit of God? " I saw, on the other hand, how much security had grown upon the men of our time, as if there were nothing to cause them fear. These things, therefore, and many more which for brevity's sake we have determined to omit, I revolved again and again in my amazed mind with compunction in my heart, and I thought to myself, "If God's peculiar people, chosen from all the people of the world, the royal seed, and holy nation, to whom he had said, 'My first begotten Israel, ' its priests, prophets, and kings, throughout so many ages, his servant and apostle, and the members of his primitive church, were not spared when the deviated from the right path, what will he do to the darkness of this our age, in which, besides all the huge and heinous sins, which it has common with all the wicked of the world committed, is found an innate, indelible, and irremediable load of folly and inconstancy? " "What, wretched man (I say to myself) is it given to you, as if you were an illustrious and learned teacher, to oppose the force of so violent a torrent, and keep the charge committed to you against such a series of inveterate crimes which has spread far and wide, without inter-ruption, for so many years? Hold thy peace: to do otherwise, is to tell the foot to see, and the hand to speak. Britain has rulers, and she has watchmen: why dost thou incline thyself thus uselessly to prate? " She has such, I say, not too many, perhaps, but surely not too few: but, because they are bent down and pressed beneath so heavy a burden, they have not time allowed them to take breath. My senses, therefore, as if feeling a portion of my debt and obligation, preoccupied themselves with such objections, and with others yet more strong. They struggled, as I said, no short time, in fearful strait, whilst I read, "There is a time for speaking, and a time for keeping silence. " At length, the creditor's side prevailed and bore off the victory: if (said he) thou art not bold enough to be marked with the comely mark of golden liberty among the prophetic creatures, who enjoy the rank as reasoning beings next to the angels, refuse not the inspiration of the understanding ass, to that day dumb, which would not carry forward the tiara'd magician who was going to curse God's people, but in the narrow pass of the vineyard crushed his loosened foot, and thereby felt the lash; and though he was, with his ungrateful and furious hand, against right justice, beating her innocent sides, she pointed out to him the heavenly messenger holding the naked sword, and standing in his way, though he had not seen him.]

* Notwithstanding this remark of Gildas, the Britons must have shown great bravery and resolution in their battles against the Saxons, or they would not have resisted their encroachments so Long. When Gildas was writing, a hundred years had elapsed, and The Britons still possessed a large portion of their native country.

Wherefore in zeal for the house of God and for his holy law, constrained either by the reasonings of my own thoughts, or by the pious entreaties of my brethren, I now discharge the debt so long exacted of me; humble, indeed, in style, but faithful, as I think, and friendly to all Christ's youthful soldiers, but severe and insupportable to foolish apostates; the former of whom, if I am not deceived, will receive the same with tears flowing from god's love; but the others with sorrow, such as is extorted from the indignation and pusillanimity of a convicted conscience.

2. I will, therefore, if God be willing, endeavour to say a few words about the situation of Britain, her disobedience and subjection, her rebellion, second subjection and dreadful slavery—of her religion, persecution, holy martyrs, heresies of different kinds —of her tyrants, her two hostile and ravaging nations—of her first devastation, her defence, her second devastation, and second taking vengeance—of her third devastation, of her famine, and the letters to Agitius*-of her victory and her crimes—of the sudden rumour of enemies—of her famous pestilence-of her counsels —of her last enemy, far more cruel than the first-of the subversion of her cities, and of the remnant that escaped; and finally, of the peace which, by the will of God, has been granted her in these our times.

* Or Aetius

II. The History

3. The island of Britain, situated on almost the utmost border of the earth, towards the south and west, and poised in the divine balance, as it is said, which supports the whole world, stretches out from the south-west towards the north pole, and is eight hundred miles long and two hundred broad[1], except where the headlands of sundry promontories stretch farther into the sea. It is surrounded by the ocean, which forms winding bays, and is strongly defended by this ample, and, if I may so call it, impassable barrier, save on the south side, where the narrow sea affords a passage to Belgic Gaul. It is enriched by the mouths of two noble rivers, the Thames and the Severn, as it were two arms, by which foreign luxuries were of old imported, and by other streams of less importance. It is famous for eight and twenty cities, and is embellished by certain castles, with walls, towers, well barred gates, and houses with threatening battlements built on high, and provided with all requisite instruments of defence. Its plains are spacious, its hills are pleasantly situated, adapted for superior tillage, and its mountains are admirably calculated for the alternate pasturage of cattle, where flowers of various colours, trodden by the feet of man, give it the appearance of a lovely picture. It is decked, like a man's chosen bride, with divers jewels, with lucid fountains and abundant

brooks wandering over the snow white sands; with transparent rivers, flowing in gentle murmurs, and offering a sweet pledge of slumber[2] to those who recline upon their banks, whilst it is irrigated by abundant lakes, which pour forth cool torrents of refreshing water.

[1] The description of Britain is given in very nearly the same terms, by Orosius, Bede, and others, but the numbers denoting the length and breadth and other dimensions, are different in almost every MS. Copy.

[2] "Soporem" in some MSS., "saporem" in others; it is difficult from the turgidity and superabundance of the style to determine which is the best meaning.

4. This island, stiff—necked and stubborn—minded, from the time of its being first inhabited, ungratefully rebels, sometimes against God, sometimes against her own citizens, and frequently also, against foreign kings and their subjects. For what can there either be, or be committed, more disgraceful or more unrighteous in human affairs, than to refuse to show fear to God or affection to one's own countrymen, and (without detriment to one's faith) to refuse due honour to those of higher dignity, to cast off all regard to reason, human and divine, and, in contempt of heaven and earth, to be guided by one's own sensual inventions? I shall, therefore, omit those ancient errors common to all the

nations of the earth, in which, before Christ came in the flesh, all mankind were bound; nor shall I enumerate those diabolical idols of my country, which almost surpassed in number those of Egypt, and of which we still see some mouldering away within or without the deserted temples, with stiff and deformed features as was customary. Nor will I call out upon the mountains, fountains, or hills, or upon the rivers, which now are subservient to the use of men, but once were an abomination and destruction to them, and to which the blind people paid divine honour. I shall also pass over the bygone times of our cruel tyrants, whose notoriety was spread over to far distant countries; so that Porphyry, that dog who in the east was always so fierce against the church, in his mad and vain style added this also, that "Britain is a land fertile in tyrants. "* I will only endeavour to relate the evils which Britain suffered in the times of the Roman emperors, and also those which she caused to distant states; but so far as lies in my power, I shall not follow the writings and records of my own country, which (if there ever were any of them) have been consumed in the fires of the enemy, or have accompanied my exiled countrymen into distant lands, but be guided by the relations of foreign writers, which, being broken and interrupted in many places are therefore by no means clear.

* Gildas here confuses the modern idea of a tyrant with that of an usurper. The latter is a sense in which Britain was said to be fertile in tyrants, viz. In usurpers of the imperial dignity.

5. For when the rulers of Rome had obtained the empire of the world, subdued all the neighbouring nations and islands towards the east, and strengthened their renown by the first peace which they made with the Parthians, who border on India, there was a general cessation from war throughout the whole world; the fierce flame which they kindled could not be extinguished or checked by the Western Ocean, but passing beyond the sea, imposed submission upon our island without resistance, and entirely reduced to obedience its unwarlike but faithless people, not so much by fire and sword and warlike engines, like other nations, but threats alone, and menaces of judgments frowning on their countenance, whilst terror penetrated to their hearts.

6. When afterwards they returned to Rome, for want of pay, as is said, and had no suspicion of an approaching rebellion, that deceitful lioness (Boadicea) put to death the rulers who had been left among them, to unfold more fully and to confirm the enterprises of the Romans. When the report of these things reached the senate, and they with a speedy army made haste to take vengeance on the crafty foxes, * as they called them, there was no bold navy on the sea to fight bravely for the country; by land there was no marshalled army, no right wing of battle, nor other preparation for resistance; but their backs were their shields against their vanquishers, and they presented their necks to their swords, whilst chill terror ran through every limb, and they stretched out their

hands to be bound, like women; so that it has become a proverb far and wide, that the Britons are neither brave in war nor faithful in time of peace.

* The Britons who fought under Boadicea were anything but "crafty foxes. " "Bold lions" is a much more appropriate appellation; they would also have been victorious if they had half the military advantages of the Romans.

7. The Romans, therefore, having slain many of the rebels, and reserved others for slaves, that the land might not be entirely reduced to desolation, left the island, destitute as it was of wine and oil, and returned to Italy, leaving behind them taskmasters, to scourge the shoulders of the natives, to reduce their necks to the yoke, and their soil to the vassalage of a Roman province; to chastise the crafty race, not with warlike weapons, but with rods, and if necessary to gird upon their sides the naked sword, so that it was no longer thought to be Britain, but a Roman island; and all their money, whether of copper, gold, or silver, was stamped with Caesar's image.

8. Meanwhile these islands, stiff with cold and frost, and in a distant region of the world, remote from the visible

sun, received the beams of light, that is, the holy precepts of Christ, the true Sun, showing to the whole world his splendour, not only from the temporal firmament, but from the height of heaven, which surpasses every thing temporal, at the latter part, as we know, of the reign of Tiberius Caesar, by whom his religion was propagated without impediment, and death threatened to those who interfered with its professors.

9. These rays of light were received with lukewarm minds by the inhabitants, but they nevertheless took root among some of them in a greater or less degree, until the nine years' persecution of the tyrant Diocletian, when the churches throughout the whole world were overthrown, all the copies of the Holy Scriptures which could be found burned in the streets, and the chosen pastors of God's flock butchered, together with their innocent sheep, in order that not a vestige, if possible, might remain in some provinces of Christ's religion. What disgraceful flights then took place-what slaughter and death inflicted by way of punishment in divers shapes, —what dreadful apostacies from religion; and on the contrary, what glorious crowns of martyrdom then were won, —what raving fury was displayed by the persecutors, and patience on the part of the suffering saints, ecclesiastical history informs us; for the whole church were crowding in a body, to leave behind them the dark things of this world, and to make the best of

their way to the happy mansions of heaven, as if to their proper home.

10. God, therefore, who wishes all men to be saved, and who calls sinners no less than those who think themselves righteous, magnified his mercy towards us, and, as we know, during the above-named persecution, that Britain might not totally be enveloped in the dark shades of night, he, of his own free gift, kindled up among us bright luminaries of holy martyrs, whose places of burial and of martyrdom, had they not for our manifold crimes been interfered with and destroyed by the barbarians, would have still kindled in the minds of the beholders no small fire of divine charity. Such were St. Alban of Verulam, Aaron and Julius, citizens of Carlisle, * and the rest, of both sexes, who in different places stood their ground in the Christian contest.

* Or Caerleon.

11. The first of these martyrs, St. Alban, for charity's sake saved another confessor who was pursued by his persecutors, and was on the point of being seized, by hiding him in his house, and then by changing clothes with him, imitating in this example of Christ, who laid down his life for his sheep, and exposing himself in the

other's clothes to be pursued in his stead. So pleasing to God was this conduct, that between his confession and martyrdom, he was honoured with the performance of wonderful miracles in presence of the impious blasphemers who were carrying the Roman standards, and like the Israelites of old, who trod dry-foot an unfrequented path whilst the ark of the covenant stood some time on the sands in the midst of Jordan; so also the martyr, with a thousand others, opened a path across the noble river Thames, whose waters stood abrupt like precipices on either side; and seeing this, the first of his executors was stricken with awe, and from a wolf became a lamb; so that he thirsted for martyrdom, and boldly underwent that for which he thirsted. The other holy martyrs were tormented with divers sufferings, and their limbs were racked in such unheard of ways, that they, without delay, erected the trophies of their glorious martyrdom even in the gates of the city of Jerusalem. For those who survived, hid themselves in woods and deserts, and secret caves, waiting until God, who is the righteous judge of all, should reward their persecutors with judgment, and themselves with protection of their lives.

12. In less than ten years, therefore, of the above-named persecution, and when these bloody decrees began to fail in consequence of the death of their authors, all Christ's young disciples, after so long and wintry a night, begin to behold the genial light of heaven. They rebuild the

churches, which had been levelled to the ground; they found, erect, and finish churches to the holy martyrs, and everywhere show their ensigns as token of their victory; festivals are celebrated and sacraments received with clean hearts and lips, and all the church's sons rejoice as it were in the fostering bosom of a mother. For this holy union remained between Christ their head and the members of his church, until the Arian treason, fatal as a serpent, and vomiting its poison from beyond the sea, caused deadly dissension between brothers inhabiting the same house, and thus, as if a road were made across the sea, like wild beasts of all descriptions, and darting the poison of every heresy from their jaws, they inflicted dreadful wounds upon their country, which is ever desirous to hear something new, and remains constant long to nothing.

13. At length also, new races of tyrants sprang up, in terrific numbers, and the island, still bearing its Roman name, but casting off her institutes and laws, sent forth among the Gauls that bitter scion of her own planting Maximus, with a great number of followers, and the ensigns of royalty, which he bore without decency and without lawful right, but in a tyrannical manner, and amid the disturbances of the seditious soldiery. He, by cunning arts rather than by valour, attaching to his rule, by perjury and falsehood, all the neighbouring towns and provinces, against the Roman state, extended one of his wings to Spain, the other to Italy, fixed the seat of his

unholy government at Treves, and so furiously pushed his rebellion against his lawful emperors that he drove one of them out of Rome, and caused the other to terminate his most holy life. Trusting to these successful attempts, he not long after lost his accursed head before the walls of Aquileia, whereas he had before cut off the crowned heads of almost all the world.

14. After this, Britain is left deprived of all her soldiery and armed bands, of her cruel governors, and of the flower of her youth, who went with Maximus, but never again returned; and utterly ignorant as she was of the art of war, groaned in amazement for many years under the cruelty of two foreign nations—the Scots from the north-west, and the Picts from the north.

15. The Britons, impatient at the assaults of the Scots and Picts, their hostilities and dreadful oppressions, send ambassadors to Rome with letters, entreating in piteous terms the assistance of an armed band to protect them, and offering loyal and ready submission to the authority of Rome, if they only would expel their foes. A legion is immediately sent, forgetting their past rebellion, and provided sufficiently with arms. When they had crossed over the sea and landed, they came at once to close conflict with their cruel enemies, and slew great numbers

of them. All of them were driven beyond the borders, and the humiliated natives rescued from the bloody slavery which awaited them. By the advice of their protectors, they now built a wall across the island from one sea to the other, which being manned with a proper force, might be a terror to the foes whom it was intended to repel, and a protection to their friends whom it covered. But this wall, being made of turf instead of stone, was of no use to that foolish people, who had no head to guide them.

16. The Roman legion had no sooner returned home in joy and triumph, than their former foes, like hungry and ravening wolves, rushing with greedy jaws upon the fold which is left without a shepherd, and wafted both by the strength of oarsmen and the blowing wind, break through the boundaries, and spread slaughter on every side, and like mowers cutting down the ripe corn, they cut up, tread under foot, and overrun the whole country.

17. And now again they send suppliant ambassadors, with their garments rent and their heads covered with ashes, imploring assistance from the Romans, and like timorous chickens, crowding under the protecting wings of their parents, that their wretched country might not altogether be destroyed, and that the Roman name,

which now was but an empty sound to fill the ear, might not become a reproach even to distant nations. Upon this, the Romans, moved with compassion, as far as human nature can be, at the relations of such horrors, send forward, like eagles in their flight, their unexpected bands of cavalry by land and mariners by sea, and planting their terrible swords upon the shoulders of their enemies, they mow them down like leaves which fall at the destined period; and as a mountain-torrent swelled with numerous streams, and bursting its banks with roaring noise, with foaming crest and yeasty wave rising to the stars, by whose eddying currents our eyes are as it were dazzled, does with one of its billows overwhelm every obstacle in its way, so did our illustrious defenders vigorously drive our enemies' band beyond the sea, if any could so escape them; for it was beyond those same seas that they transported, year after year, the plunder which they had gained, no one daring to resist them.

18. The Romans, therefore, left the country, giving notice that they could no longer be harassed by such laborious expeditions, nor suffer the Roman standards, with so large and brave an army, to be worn out by sea and land by fighting against these unwarlike, plundering vagabonds; but that the islanders, inuring themselves to warlike weapons, and bravely fighting, should valiantly protect their country, their property, wives and children, and, what is dearer than these, their liberty and lives; that they should not suffer their hands to be tied behind their

backs by a nation which, unless they were enervated by idleness and sloth, was not more powerful than themselves, but that they should arm those hands with buckler, sword, and spear, ready for the field of battle; and, because they thought this also of advantage to the people they were about to leave, they, with the help of the miserable natives, built a wall different from the former, by public and private contributions, and of the same structure as walls generally, extending in a straight line from sea to sea, between some cities, which, from fear of their enemies, had there by chance been built. They then give energetic counsel to the timorous natives, and leave them patterns by which to manufacture arms. Moreover, on the south coast where their vessels lay, as there was some apprehension lest the barbarians might land, they erected towers at stated intervals, commanding a prospect of the sea; and then left the island never to return.

19. No sooner were they gone, than the Picts and Scots, like worms which in the heat of the mid-day come forth from their holes, hastily land again from their canoes, in which they had been carried beyond the Cichican* valley, differing one from another in manners, but inspired with the same avidity for blood, and all more eager to shroud their villainous faces in bushy hair than to cover with decent clothing those parts of their body which required it. Moreover, having heard of the departure of our friends, and their resolution never to return, they seized

with greater boldness than before on all the country towards the extreme north as far as the wall. To oppose them there was placed on the heights a garrison equally slow to fight and ill adapted to run away, a useless and panic-struck company, who slumbered away days and nights on their unprofitable watch. Meanwhile the hooked weapons of their enemies were not idle, and our wretched countrymen were dragged from the wall and dashed against the ground. Such premature death, however, painful as it was, saved them from seeing the miserable sufferings of their brothers and children. But why should I say more? They left their cities, abandoned the protection of the wall, and dispersed themselves in flight more desperately than before. The enemy, on the other hand, pursued them with more unrelenting cruelty than before, and butchered our countrymen like sheep, so that their habitations were like those of savage beasts; for they turned their arms upon each other, and for the sake of a little sustenance, imbrued their hands in the blood of their fellow countrymen. Thus foreign calamities were augmented by domestic feuds; so that the whole country was entirely destitute of provisions, save such as could be procured in the chase.

* The meaning of this expression is not known. O'Connor thinks it is the Irish Sea.

20. Again, therefore, the wretched remnant, sending to Aetius, a powerful Roman citizen, address him as follow:

—"To Aetius, * now consul for the third time: the groans of the Britons. " And again a little further, thus: —"The barbarians drive us to the sea; the sea throws us back on the barbarians: thus two modes of death await us, we are either slain or drowned. " The Romans, however, could not assist them, and in the meantime the discomfited people, wandering in the woods, began to feel the effects of a severe famine, which compelled many of them without delay to yield themselves up to their cruel persecutors, to obtain subsistence: others of them, however, lying hid in mountains, caves and woods, continually sallied out from thence to renew the war. And then it was, for the first time, that they overthrew their enemies, who had for so many years been living in their country; for their trust was not in man, but in God; according to the maxim of Philo, "We must have divine assistance, when that of man fails. " The boldness of the enemy was for a while checked, but not the wickedness of our countrymen; the enemy left our people, but the people did not leave their sins.

* Or Agitius, according to another reading.

21. For it has always been a custom with our nation, as it is at present, to be impotent in repelling foreign foes, but bold and invincible in raising civil war, and bearing the burdens of their offences: they are impotent, I say, in following the standard of peace and truth, but bold in wickedness and falsehood. The audacious invaders

therefore return to their winter quarters, determined before long again to return and plunder. And then, too, the Picts for the first time seated themselves at the extremity of the island, where they afterwards continued, occasionally plundering and wasting the country. During these truces, the wounds of the distressed people are healed, but another sore, still more venomous, broke out. No sooner were the ravages of the enemy checked, than the island was deluged with a most extraordinary plenty of all things, greater than was before known, and with it grew up every kind of luxury and licentiousness. It grew with so firm a root, that one might truly say of it, "Such fornication is heard of among you, as never was known the like among the Gentiles. " But besides this vice, there arose also every other, to which human nature is liable and in particular that hatred of truth, together with her supporters, which still at present destroys every thing good in the island; the love of falsehood, together with its inventors, the reception of crime in the place of virtue, the respect shown to wickedness rather than goodness, the love of darkness instead of the sun, the admission of Satan as an angel of light. Kings were anointed, not according to god's ordinance, but such as showed themselves more cruel than the rest; and soon after, they were put to death by those who had elected them, without any inquiry into their merits, but because others still more cruel were chosen to succeed them. If any one of these was of a milder nature than the rest, or in any way more regardful of the truth, he was looked upon as the ruiner of the country, every body cast a dart at him, and they valued things alike whether pleasing or displeasing to God, unless it so happened that what displeased him was pleasing to themselves. So that the words of the prophet, addressed to the people of old, might well be applied to our own countrymen: "Children without a law, have ye left God and provoked to anger the holy one of Israel? * Why will ye still inquire, adding iniquity? Every head is languid and every heart is sad; from the sole of the foot to the crown, there is no health in him. " And thus they did all things contrary to their salvation, as if no remedy could be applied to the world by the true Physician of all men. And not only the laity did so, but our Lord's own flock and its shepherds, who ought to have been an example to the people, slumbered away their time in drunkenness, as if they had been dipped in wine; whilst the swellings of pride, the jar of strife, the griping talons of envy, and the confused estimate of right and wrong, got such entire possession of the, that there seemed to be poured out (and the same still continueth) contempt upon princes, and to be made by their vanities to wander astray and not in the way.

* Isa. I. 4,5. In most of these quotations there is great verbal variation from the authorised version: the author probably quoted from memory, if not from the Latin version.

22. Meanwhile, God being willing to purify his family who were infected by so deep a stain of woe, and at the hearing only of their calamities to amend them; a vague rumour suddenly as if on wings reaches the ears of all,

that their inveterate foes were rapidly approaching to destroy the whole country, and to take possession of it, as of old, from one end to the other. But yet they derived no advantage from this intelligence; for, like frantic beasts, taking the bit of reason between their teeth, they abandoned the safe and narrow road, and rushed forward upon the broad downward path of vice, which leads to death. Whilst, therefore, as Solomon says, the stubborn servant is not cured by words, the fool is scourged and feels it not: a pestilential disease morally affected the foolish people, which, without the sword, cut off so large a number of persons, that the living were not able to bury them. But even this was no warning to them, that in them also might be fulfilled the words of Isaiah the prophet, "And God hath called his people to lamentation, to baldness, and to the girdle of sackcloth; behold they begin to kill calves, and to slay rams, to eat, to drink, and to say, 'We will eat and drink, for to-morrow we shall die. '" For the time was approaching, when all their iniquities, as formerly those of the Amorrhaeans, should be fulfilled. For a council was called to settle what was best and most expedient to be done, in order to repel such frequent and fatal irruptions and plunderings of the above-named nations.

23. Then all the councillors, together with that proud tyrant Gurthrigern [Vortigern], the British king, were so blinded, that, as a protection to their country, they sealed its doom by inviting in among them like wolves into the

sheep-fold), the fierce and impious Saxons, a race hateful both to God and men, to repel the invasions of the northern nations. Nothing was ever so pernicious to our country, nothing was ever so unlucky. What palpable darkness must have enveloped their minds-darkness desperate and cruel! Those very people whom, when absent, they dreaded more than death itself, were invited to reside, as one may say, under the selfsame roof. Foolish are the princes, as it is said, of Thafneos, giving counsel to unwise Pharaoh. A multitude of whelps came forth from the lair of this barbaric lioness, in three cyuls, as they call them, that is, in there ships of war, with their sails wafted by the wind and with omens and prophecies favourable, for it was foretold by a certain soothsayer among them, that they should occupy the country to which they were sailing three hundred years, and half of that time, a hundred and fifty years, should plunder and despoil the same. They first landed on the eastern side of the island, by the invitation of the unlucky king, and there fixed their sharp talons, apparently to fight in favour of the island, but alas! more truly against it. Their mother-land, finding her first brood thus successful, sends forth a larger company of her wolfish offspring, which sailing over, join themselves to their bastard-born comrades. From that time the germ of iniquity and the root of contention planted their poison amongst us, as we deserved, and shot forth into leaves and branches. the barbarians being thus introduced as soldiers into the island, to encounter, as they falsely said, any dangers in defence of their hospitable entertainers, obtain an allowance of provisions, which, for some time being plentifully bestowed, stopped their doggish mouths. Yet they complain that their monthly supplies are not furnished in sufficient abundance, and they industriously aggravate each occasion of quarrel, saying that unless more liberality is shown them, they will break the treaty and plunder the whole island. In a short time, they follow up their threats with deeds.

24. For the fire of vengeance, justly kindled by former crimes, spread from sea to sea, fed by the hands of our foes in the east, and did not cease, until, destroying the neighbouring towns and lands, it reached the other side of the island, and dipped its red and savage tongue in the western ocean. In these assaults, therefore, not unlike that of the Assyrian upon Judea, was fulfilled in our case what the prophet describes in words of lamentation; "They have burned with fire the sanctuary; they have polluted on earth the tabernacle of thy name. " And again, "O God, the gentiles have come into thine inheritance; thy holy temple have they defiled, " &c. So that all the columns were levelled with the ground by the frequent strokes of the battering-ram, all the husbandmen routed, together with their bishops, priests, and people, whilst the sword gleamed, and the flames crackled around them on every side. Lamentable to behold, in the midst of the streets lay the tops of lofty towers, tumbled to the ground, stones of high walls, holy altars, fragments of human bodies, covered with livid clots of coagulated blood, looking as if they had been squeezed together in a press; * and with no chance of

being buried, save in the ruins of the houses, or in the ravening bellies of wild beasts and birds; with reverence be it spoken for their blessed souls, if, indeed, there were many found who were carried, at that time, into the high heaven by the holy angels. So entirely had the vintage, once so fine, degenerated and become bitter, that, in the words of the prophet, there was hardly a grape or ear of corn to be seen where the husbandman had turned his back.

25. Some therefore, of the miserable remnant, being taken in the mountains, were murdered in great numbers; others, constrained by famine, came and yielded themselves to be slaves for ever to their foes, running the risk of being instantly slain, which truly was the greatest favour that could be offered them: some others passed beyond the seas with loud lamentations instead of the voice of exhortation. "Thou hast given us as sheep to be slaughtered, and among the Gentiles hast thou dispersed us. " Others, committing the safeguard of their lives, which were in continual jeopardy, to the mountains, precipices, thickly wooded forests, and to the rocks of the seas (albeit with trembling hearts), remained still in their country. But in the meanwhile, an opportunity happening, when these most cruel robbers were returned home, the poor remnants of our nation (to whom flocked from divers places round about our miserable countrymen as fast as bees to their hives, for fear of an ensuing storm), being strengthened by God, calling upon

him with all their hearts, as the poet says, —"With their unnumbered vows they burden heaven, " that they might not be brought to utter destruction, took arms under the conduct of Ambrosius Aurelianus, a modest man, who of all the Roman nation was then alone in the confusion of this troubled period by chance left alive. His parents, who for their merit were adorned with the purple, had been slain in these same broils, and now his progeny in these our days, although shamefully degenerated from the worthiness of their ancestors, provoke to battle their cruel conquerors, and by the goodness of our Lord obtain the victory.

26. After this, sometimes our countrymen, sometimes the enemy, won the field, to the end that our Lord might in this land try after his accustomed manner these his Israelites, whether they loved him or not, until the year of the siege of Bath-hill, when took place also the last almost, though not the least slaughter of our cruel foes, which was (as I am sure) forty-four years and one month after the landing of the Saxons, and also the time of my own nativity. And yet neither to this day are the cities of our country inhabited as before, but being forsaken and overthrown, still lie desolate; our foreign wars having ceased, but our civil troubles still remaining. For as well the remembrance of such terrible desolation of the island, as also of the unexpected recovery of the same, remained in the minds of those who were eyewitnesses of the wonderful events of both, and in regard thereof, kings,

public magistrates, and private persons, with priests and clergymen, did all and every one of them live orderly according to their several vocations. But when these had departed out of this world, and a new race succeeded, who were ignorant of this troublesome time, and had only experience of the present prosperity, all the laws of truth and justice were so shaken and subverted, that not so much as a vestige or remembrance of these virtues remained among the above-named orders of men, except among a very few who, compared with the great multitude which were daily rushing headlong down to hell, are accounted so small a number, that our reverend mother, the church, scarcely beholds them, her only true children, reposing in her bosom; whose worthy lives, being a pattern to al men, and beloved of God, inasmuch as by their holy prayers, as by certain pillars and most profitable supporters, our infirmity is sustained up, that it may not utterly be broken down, I would have no one suppose I intended to reprove, if forced by the increasing multitude of offences, I have freely, aye, with anguish, not so much declared as bewailed the wickedness of those who are become servants, not only to their bellies, but also to the devil rather than to Christ, who is our blessed God, world without end.

Lightning Source UK Ltd.
Milton Keynes UK
UKHW041139070122
396761UK00001B/2